W9-CLJ-065

Pebble® Plus

AFRICAN ANIMALS

Zebras

by Catherine Ipcizade

Consulting Editor: Gail Saunders-Smith, PhD

Consultant:
George Wittemyer, PhD
NSF International Postdoctoral Fellow
University of California at Berkeley

Capstone press®

Mankato, Minnesota

Pebble Plus is published by Capstone Press,
1710 Roe Crest Drive, North Mankato, Minnesota 56003.
www.capstonepub.com

Library of Congress Cataloging-in-Publication Data
Ipcizade, Catherine.
   Zebras / by Catherine Ipcizade.
   p. cm. — (Pebble plus. African animals)
   Includes bibliographical references and index.
   ISBN-13: 978-1-4296-1251-7 (library binding)
   ISBN-13: 978-1-4296-4885-1 (paperback)
   1. Zebras — Africa — Juvenile literature. I. Title. II. Series.
QL737.U62I63 2008
599.665'7 — dc22   2007028773

Summary: Discusses zebras, their African habitat, food, and behavior.

Editorial Credits
Erika L. Shores, editor; Renée T. Doyle, set designer; Laura Manthe, photo researcher

Photo Credits
Afripics.com, 10–11
Brand X Pictures/John Lambert, cover, 22
Getty Images Inc./Jonathan & Angela, 6–7
iStockphoto/Hansjoerg Richter, 12–13
Peter Arnold Inc./Gunter Ziesler, 18–19
Photodisc/Siede Preis, cover, 1, 3 (fur)
Shutterstock/Clement K. L. Cheah, 14–15; Duncan Gilbert, 5; Geir Olav Lyngfjell, 8–9; SouWest Photography, 17
Tom & Pat Leeson, 20–21

**The author dedicates this book to her parents — all of them. Thank you for your encouragement,
    support, and love.**

Note to Parents and Teachers

The African Animals set supports national science standards related to life science. This
book describes and illustrates zebras. The images support early readers in understanding
the text. The repetition of words and phrases helps early readers learn new words.
This book also introduces early readers to subject-specific vocabulary words, which are
defined in the Glossary section. Early readers may need assistance to read some words
and to use the Table of Contents, Glossary, Read More, Internet Sites, and Index sections
of the book.

Printed in the United States of America in Eau Claire, Wisconsin.
062013
007562R

Table of Contents

Living in Africa

Zebras live in Africa.

They graze on grass

growing on the savanna.

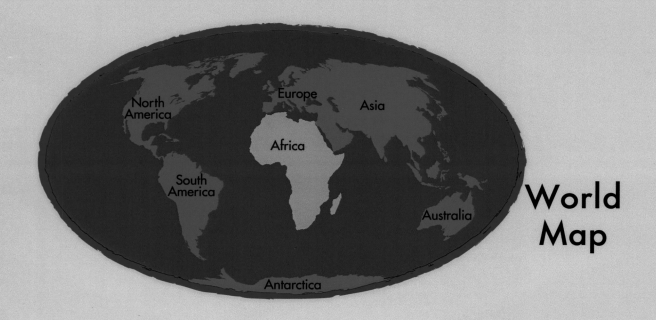

World Map

Zebras live together in herds.
Thousands of zebras can
make up one herd.

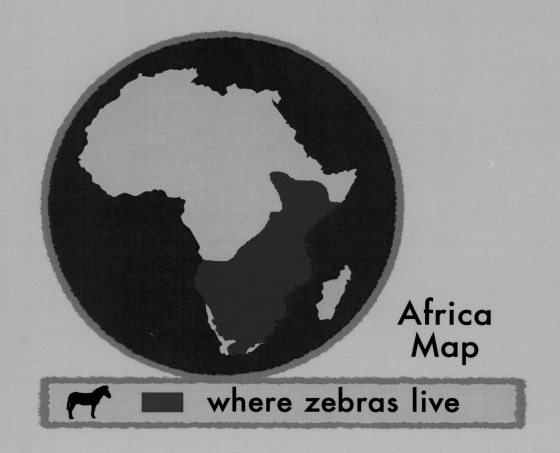

Africa
Map

🐎 ▇ where zebras live

Up Close!

Zebras look like
striped horses.
No two zebras have
the same stripe pattern.

Even a zebra's mane
has stripes.
The black and white hair
sticks up on its neck.

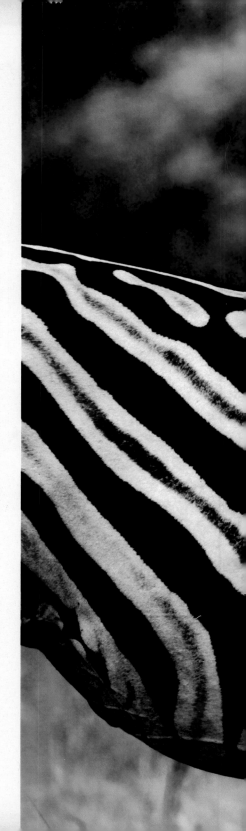

A zebra's eyes are far apart.

It can look for danger

all around.

Eating and Drinking

A zebra's sharp teeth

snip tall grasses.

Zebras graze all day.

Slurp!

Zebras are never far

from water.

They need to drink water

every day.

Staying Safe

Lions and hyenas hunt zebras.

Zebras run fast to get away.

Adult zebras sleep standing up.
They are ready to run
at the first sign of danger.
Good night, zebras.

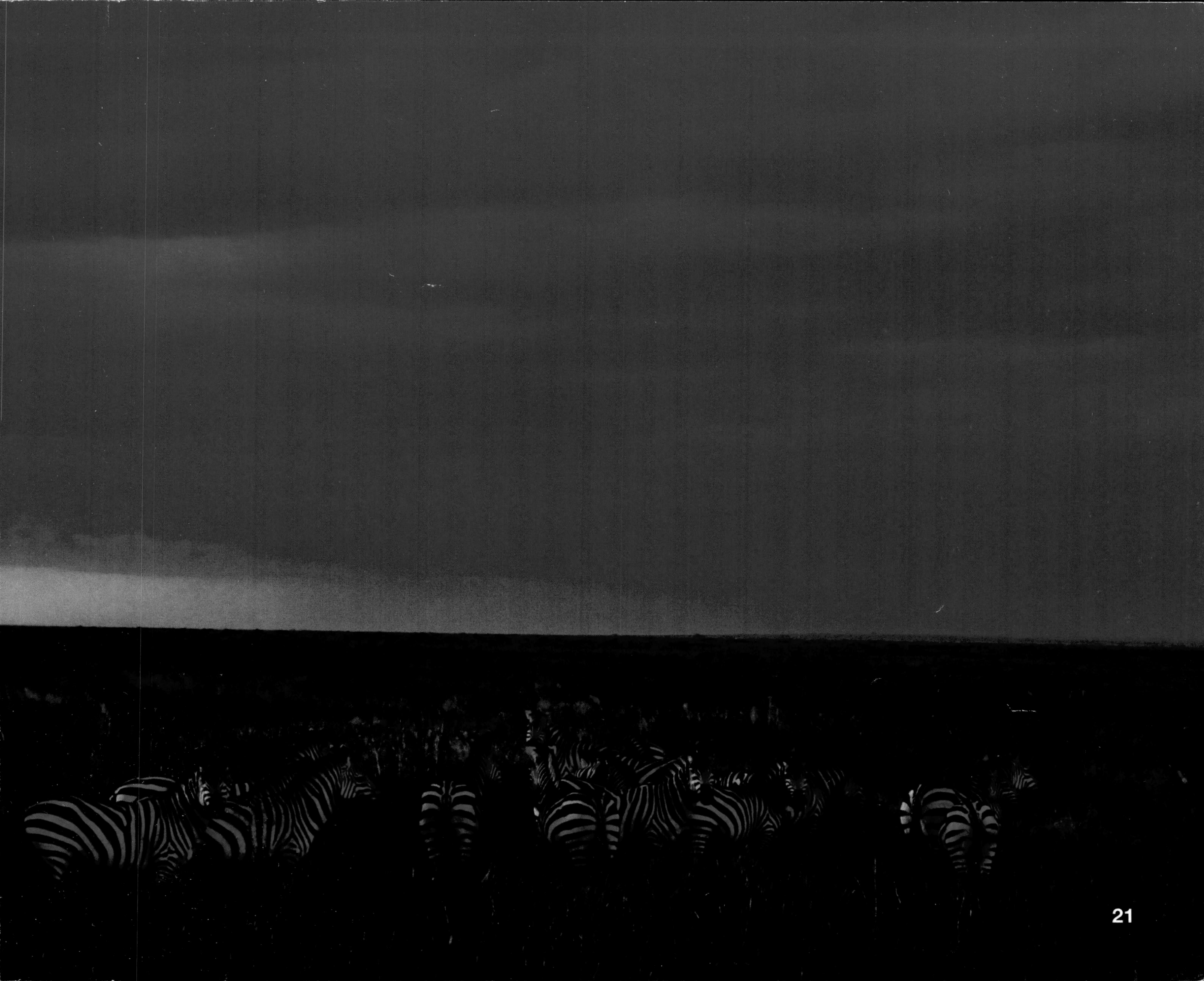

Glossary

danger — something that is not safe

graze — to eat grass and other plants

herd — a group of the same kind of animal that lives together

mane — long, thick hair that grows on the head and neck of some animals

pattern — a repeating order of colors and shapes

savanna — a flat, grassy plain with few trees

Read More

Murray, Julie. *Zebras.* A Buddy Book. Animal Kingdom. Edina, Minn.: Abdo, 2003.

Whitehouse, Patricia. *Zebra.* Heinemann Read and Learn. Zoo Animals. Chicago: Heinemann, 2003.

Internet Sites

FactHound offers a safe, fun way to find Internet sites related to this book. All of the sites on FactHound have been researched by our staff.

Here's how:

1. Visit www.facthound.com

2. Choose your grade level.

3. Type in this book ID 1429612517 for age-appropriate sites. You may also browse subjects by clicking on letters, or by clicking on pictures and words.

4. Click on the Fetch It button.

FactHound will fetch the best sites for you!

Index

Word Count: 122
Grade: 1
Early-Intervention Level: 18